# Ford GT40 MkIII (1967)

Ford's race car version of the GT40 humiliated Ferrari at Le Mans in the latter half of the 1960s. It also spawned a road-going version in 1967 that was panned by critics for its sloppy road manners. But real drivers didn't care about its manners, because the GT40 MkIII could see off its competitors in a straight line with the 306bhp produced by its 4.7-litre V8 engine – and boasted 0-60 in 5.5secs. Its top speed of 170mph also hinted at what the future held for true supercars. Only seven GT40s (MkIII) were ever built.

## Specifications:

| | |
|---|---|
| Engine | 4736cc |
| Max power | 306bhp at 6,000rpm |
| Max torque | 229lb ft at 4,200rpm |
| 0-60mph | 5.5secs |
| Top speed | 170mph |

SPP 604D

## Lamborghini Muira (1966–1972)

Unveiled to a stunned audience at the Geneva Motor Show, Switzerland, in 1966, the Muira is what many believe to be the planet's first true supercar, partly because its mid-mounted engine was a world first. Just as importantly, the engine's placement had a direct effect on the car's appearance – and those looks are still stunning. The greatest version of Muira is the SV produced at the beginning of the 1970s, which saw the original's 350bhp increased to 385bhp. The only problem with the Muira is that the front end is prone to lift at high speeds because of the engine layout – so handle with care.

**Lamborghini Muira SV specifications (1971–1972):**

| | |
|---|---|
| Engine | 3929cc |
| Max power | 385bhp at 7,850rpm |
| Max torque | 294lb ft at 5,750rpm |
| 0-60mph | 6.0secs |
| Top speed | 180mph |

*Other key cars from the 1960s:*
*Jaguar E-Type, Ferrari 275 GTB, Ferrari 365 GTB Daytona, Corvette Sting Ray, De Tomaso Mangusta.*

*Lamborghini Countach 25th Anniversary (1989–1990)*

# Lamborghini Countach (1974–1990)

It's one of the defining shapes in car history – the prototype Countach, which was shown for the first time in 1971, was greeted with rapture by the crowds. The replacement for the Muira, the sleek, sensual lines had been supplanted with dramatic lines and a wedge shape that would come to dominate the supercar world for the next ten years. The first Lamborghini Countach to be released (the LP400) featured a 3.9-litre V12 engine that could make the sprint from 0-60 in 5.6secs. Several incarnations of the Countach, which included the celebrated 5-litre Countach QV in 1985, followed over its illustrious 17-year reign as the king of the supercars. It has to be said though that the Countach represents the ultimate old-school supercar – it offered a driving experience that had to be learned; simply getting behind the wheel and flooring it was not to be recommended. After all, you can't tame a bull.

### LP400 specifications (1974–1982):

| | |
|---|---|
| Engine | 3929cc |
| Max power | 375bhp at 8,000rpm |
| Max torque | 268lbft at 5,000rpm |
| 0-60mph | 5.6secs |
| Top speed | 180mph + |

## BMW M1
## (1978-1981)

The M1 is one of the unsung heroes of the 1970s. It was BMW's first (and, so far, only) foray into creating a mid-engined supercar, and it could have worked out if the project hadn't been besieged by problems. It was intended that the M1 would be styled and built by Lamborghini, but because the raging bull was experiencing money woes, Bauer, in Germany, produced the car for BMW. More trouble was to strike – the car had been intended for the track but these plans fell through. It's a tragedy because the road-going M1 put the wind up its Italian rivals by offering the same levels of grip but pairing it with forgiving handling and bullet-proof reliability – not exactly a forte of Italian supercars at the time.

**Specifications:**

| | |
|---|---|
| Engine | 3453cc |
| Max power | 277bhp at 6,500rpm |
| Max torque | 243lb ft at 5,000rpm |
| 0-60mph | 5.6secs |
| Top speed | 162mph |

*Other key cars from the 1970s: Maserati Bora, Porsche 911 2.7 RS, Porsche 911 Turbo, Aston Martin V8 Vantage.*

*Lotus Turbo Esprit SE (1989)*

# Lotus Turbo Esprit (1980-1992)

The Lotus Esprit has had a long and illustrious history dating back to when the car was first introduced in 1976. One of the most revered versions was the Turbo that first surfaced in 1980 and featured a four-cylinder aluminium engine that could produce 210bhp. The Esprit's 'credentials' were further increased thanks to a movie appearance – the Turbo was James Bond's vehicle of choice (both on the road and underwater) in The Spy Who Loved Me. Over the decades there have been numerous incarnations of the Esprit, but its production run (that spanned an incredible 28 years) came to a close on February 21st, 2004. Fans needn't worry though – Lotus are already designing its replacement.

**Specifications:**

| | |
|---|---|
| Engine | 2174cc |
| Max power | 210bhp at 6,250rpm |
| Max torque | 200lb ft at 4,500rpm |
| 0-60mph | 5.6secs |
| Top speed | 150mph |

## Ferrari 288 GTO (1984–1985)

The mid-engined GTO is actually the forefather of the classic F40, but this 1980s supercar has earned its rightful place in the history books because its body was manufactured from composite materials such as carbon fibre – making it one of the very few cars to feature such race-developed technology. These lightweight materials coupled with a twin-turbo 2.8-litre V8 engine meant that the GTO was an extremely quick car with handling that was, let's just say, best exploited by the 'experienced driver'.

### Specifications:

| | |
|---|---|
| Engine | 2855cc |
| Max power | 400bhp at 7,000rpm |
| Max torque | 466lb ft at 3,800rpm |
| 0-60mph | 4.7secs |
| Top speed | 188mph |

## Ferrari Testarossa (1984–1992)

Aimed at being more of a GT than a hardcore road racer, the Testarossa ('Red Head') showed Ferrari heading in a more refined direction while retaining the astonishing speed and acceleration that all supercar owners demand. And the flat-12 engine saw to that with its 390bhp.

### Specifications:

| | |
|---|---|
| Engine | 4942cc |
| Max power | 390bhp at 6,300rpm |
| Max torque | 354lb ft at 4,500rpm |
| 0-60mph | 5.3secs |
| Top speed | 180mph |

## *Porsche 959 (1987–1991)*

Trust Porsche to come up with a world-class supercar – the 959 was able to hit 0-60 in under 4secs. This phenomenal acceleration was achieved with typical German efficiency using a rear-mounted twin-turbo flat-six engine that produced 450bhp. To get such power down onto the road, the 959 featured four-wheel drive paired with a six-speed gearbox, and the kind of stability needed to hit a cool 197mph.

**Specifications:**

| | |
|---|---|
| Engine | 2850cc |
| Max power | 450bhp at 6,500rpm |
| Max torque | 369lb ft at 5,000rpm |
| 0-60mph | 3.6secs |
| Top speed | 197mph |

*Other key cars from the 1980s:*
*Aston Martin Bulldog, Aston Martin*
*Vantage Zagato, Ruf CTR Yellowbird.*

## *Ferrari F40 (1987–1992)*

Released to celebrate the company's 40th anniversary, the F40 was the last road car that the marque's creator, Enzo Ferrari, commissioned before he passed away – but what a swansong. It looked more like a racing car than a supercar and it featured a 2.9-litre V8 engine that would see a brave driver propelled to over 200mph. The car is, of course, not for the faint-hearted but its position as one of the iconic supercars of any age is indisputable.

**Specifications:**

| | |
|---|---|
| Engine | 2936cc |
| Max power | 478bhp at 7,000rpm |
| Max torque | 425lb ft at 4,000rpm |
| 0-60mph | 3.9secs |
| Top speed | 201mph |

## Bugatti EB110 (1992–1995)

It was supposed to be the rebirth of the Bugatti brand and, at first, the future was looking bright for the marque. While the EB110's looks may have been controversial, the Bugatti was a true supercar with staggering performance; it featured, thanks to the chassis and four-wheel drive, a colossal amount of grip to make the most out of all that power. Two versions were available – the 'humble' GT with 553bhp and the Supersport which boasted 603bhp. But alas, the Bugatti dream imploded in 1995 when the company went bust, mainly because of the global recession.

### EB110 Supersport specifications:

| | |
|---|---|
| Engine | 3500cc |
| Max power | 603bhp at 8,250rpm |
| Max torque | 479lb ft at 4,250rpm |
| 0-60mph | 3.1secs |
| Top speed | 218mph |

## Jaguar XJ220 (1992–1994)

Quite frankly, the Jaguar supercar was something of a debacle. Back in 1988 customers were bedazzled by promises of a huge V12 engine, coupled with a four-wheel drive, when the XJ220 prototype was unveiled. Down went the deposits as (very rich) people waited for the car's arrival in 1992. The trouble was that Jaguar replaced the engine with a V6 and dumped the four-wheel drive. Some angry customers withdrew their orders and demanded their deposits back; legal wranglings ensued. Add to this a world recession, and Jaguar's supercar foundered. The sad fact is that on its release, the XJ220 was still a fantastically fast car boasting supreme handling (in the dry) – and then there were those striking looks.

### Specifications

| | |
|---|---|
| Engine | 2498cc |
| Max power | 542bhp at 6,500rpm |
| Max torque | 472lb ft at 5,000rpm |
| 0-60mph | 3.6secs |
| Top speed | 210mph + |

*This is what everyone is calling the new 'baby' Aston, but it's destined to make one very big splash when it finally touches down...*

It could be argued that the V8 Vantage is the single most important Aston ever to be built. While the Vanquish and DB9 are designed to be sporting GTs that can deliver extreme comfort while offering superb dynamics, the V8 Vantage is meant to be only one thing – a straight-up, no compromises sports car. It's the most affordable Aston to be made available to the masses with a price of £74,500 (US price upon application), which will put it in line with the likes of the Porsche 911.

# Aston Martin V8 Vantage

That's virgin territory for Aston Martin, but by all accounts, they are all set to hit the mark right on the bulls-eye. Using their unique aluminium VH platform, as used by the DB9 but shortened with stiffer suspension, the V8 Vantage has a howling 4.3-litre engine providing the firepower. While the V8 Vantage 'only' features a V8, it can match the V12-driven DB9 because it's lighter – giving it a 0–60 time of 4.8secs and a top speed of 175mph; the V8 Vantage owner won't feel inferior in the company of Ferrari or Lamborghini either, never mind its bigger brother.

Unsurprisingly of course, the interior of the two-seater is up to the typical Aston high standards – the alloy fascia with instrument panel features beautifully finished aluminium. But diehard wood fans won't be disappointed – like the DB9, optional mahogany, walnut or bamboo can be included.

As for the build quality, 78 prototypes have been clocking up 1,500,000 miles between them – suffering the searing temperatures of 48°C in Dubai, and enduring −30°C in Sweden. The Nürburgring, Germany, and the Nardo test track, Italy, have been used to develop and hone the V8 Vantage's handling and performance to ensure that the car delivers on its hype while not breaking down after the first quarter of a mile – in fact, one V8 Vantage was challenged with the task of racking up 5,000 miles round the Nürburgring, which it did without breaking its stride.

While it's not strictly a supercar, as is the case with all Astons, there is something about the V8 Vantage that propels it into that category – perhaps it's the perfect styling created by Henrik Fisker – that long nose, the perfect cut lines and its unquestionable presence. It's exotica defined, and put up against its competitors you have to ask yourself – which one is the more desirable? Which one has that 'X factor' which elevates it beyond mere sports car? The answer is staring you in the face...

It's perhaps telling that if this book had been written five years ago, we may have been hard pushed to feature one Aston Martin, let alone three. Perhaps the reborn Aston Martin shows that the amassed talent based in Modena, Italy, has a new direct competitor for making the ultimate exotica that boasts near-unparalleled desirability – and that new region is known as Gaydon, UK. The name will grow on you, we promise.

## Wait-y Issues...

To make sure the V8 Vantage keeps that important air of exclusivity, production of the car will be capped at 2,500 per year. Expect epic waiting lists – for the driver slapping down his deposit today, you can expect to wait until 2007 before it appears on the driveway.

## Designer Departed

The good-looking V8 Vantage was designed by Henrik Fisker (who also designed the DB9). He has since departed Aston Martin and moved to California to set up an automotive design and customization company.

## Weight A Minute...

The front-engined V8 Vantage has the spot-on weight distribution and offers the ideal set-up for any self-respecting sports car.
The Aston's dry-sump lubrication system means that the engine can be placed lower in the body, meaning a lower centre of gravity.
The result – better balance and stability.

## Aston Martin V8 Vantage: The Specifications

| | | | | | | | |
|---|---|---|---|---|---|---|---|
| Engine | All alloy quad overhead camshaft 32 valve V8 | Maximum speed | 175mph | Suspension front | Independent double aluminium wishbones with coil over aluminium monutube dampers & anti-roll bar | Length | 4383mm/173in |
| | | Steering | Rack and pinion with power assist | | | Width | 1866mm/73in |
| Valvetrain | DOHC 4 valves / cyl | | | | | Height | 1255mm/49in |
| Displacement | 4280cc | Brakes front | Ventilated & grooved steel discs with four- piston monobloc callipers/ 355mm/14in, ABS | | | Wheels front | 8.5 x 18in |
| Maximum power | 380bhp at 7,000rpm | | | Suspension rear | Independent double aluminium wishbones with coil over aluminium monutube dampers & anti-roll bar | Wheel rear | 9.5 x 18in |
| Maximum torque | 302Ib ft at 5,000rpm | | | | | Price | £74,500 US price upon applicaton |
| Transmission | Six-speed manual | Brakes rear | Ventilated & grooved steel discs with four- piston monobloc callipers/ 330mm/13in, ABS | | | | |
| 0–60mph | 4.8secs | | | Kerb weight | 1570kg/3461lbs | | |

*Is it beauty or the beast? It doesn't really matter, the Enzo defines what the supercar moniker is all about...*

Explosive, aggressive, uncompromising – these are just some of the words that roar into your mind when you first see the Ferrari Enzo. Where do you start with such bold statement in supercar design? On its release in 2002, it was perhaps intended as a boast; a flipping of the finger at all the other supercar manufacturers that had been snapping at the heels of Ferrari since the marque began making cars back in 1947.

# Ferrari Enzo

Named after the company's founder Enzo Ferrari, who died in 1988, the Enzo is the marque's fastest ever road-going car with a top speed of over 217mph, and the looks penned by Pininfarina are pure Formula One drama. There are no luscious curves that one normally associates with a exotic supercar; the Enzo makes its intent clear; that F1 nose, the angular body and those venturis shout to even the most casual of observers that this car is the closest a driver will ever get to feeling like Michael Schumacher.

But being a Ferrari, the Enzo is not all show – it also goes like a beast. With 660bhp produced by an ultra lightweight aluminium 6-litre V12 engine, the Enzo can devour many of its modern day competitors with a 0–60 time of 3.5secs. It almost has enough torque to stop the Earth rotating if you should happen to floor the gas while heading in an easterly direction.

Ferrari have made sure that the Enzo makes the most of its gigantic power by using its hi-tech ASR traction control system and an F1-style six-speed paddle shift that can snap through the gears in milliseconds. The Enzo's handling is legendary as well – its chassis is constructed from carbon fibre and Kevlar honeycomb, which provides the Enzo with its extreme rigidity and strength; while that F1 nose, with its three air intakes, helps to keep the car glued to the road as it increases in speed, while keeping the V12 cool. Stopping capability is vital for such explosive thrust – and the carbon ceramic brakes with ABS are more than a match for such a punishing job.

Open the Enzo's scissor doors and there's easy access to the carbon fibre and leather cabin. The steering wheel is a F1 fan's idea of paradise with a multitude of F1-style buttons mounted on it for controlling everything from race settings to turning off the ASR (if the driver is feeling brave enough). And for that extra Grand Prix touch, there are LEDs running along the top of the wheel, which act as a rev counter.

The Ferrari Enzo is currently regarded as the most technologically advanced supercar available. There's no question that the Enzo is an evolutionary step towards bringing road and track cars closer together. Perhaps the only concern is how Ferrari will top this.

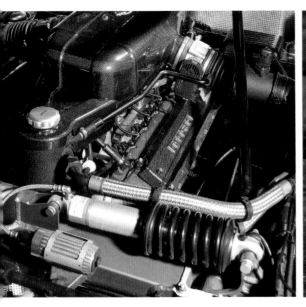

## Going, Going, Gone

Like any respectable supercar, limiting the numbers that can be bought is paramount. Initially, only 349 Enzos were made to order, and Ferrari sold every single one of them before they'd even shown a single picture or spec list of the car. The final figure for the number of Enzos assembled is 400 – one more than planned, with the extra car being auctioned off to raise money for the 2004 Asian tsunami appeal.

## F1 Champ Elevates Enzo

Formula One champion Michael Schumacher had a firm hand in developing the Enzo. He drove several prototypes of the supercar and gave his thoughts on all aspects of the Enzo, from its performance to the driving position. In fact, thanks to Schumacher, there are 16 different pedal settings available to choose from.

## Sky's The Limit

It would appear that the Enzo's value doesn't depreciate – hardly surprising considering the number Ferrari has actually ended up building. But if you want proof–in 2004, the Enzo became eBay Motors' most expensive car ever sold when a Swiss man (bidding from Brazil) made a winning bid of £544,000/US$1,038,227 – a brand new Enzo is worth £450,000/US$670,000.

## Pulling Power

A survey by the RAC Foundation, based in Britain, discovered that 86 percent of British men would rather spend the weekend with a Ferrari Enzo than hang out with former *Baywatch* star Pamela Anderson. Well, at least the Enzo features more natural materials!

## Ferrari Enzo: The Specifications

| | | | | | | | |
|---|---|---|---|---|---|---|---|
| Engine | Aluminium V12 | 0–60mph | 3.5secs | Brakes Rear | Ventilated carbon-ceramic discs with 4-pot callipers, ABS/380mm/15in | Kerb Weight | 1365kg/3009lbs |
| Valvetrain | DOHC, 4 valves /cyl with Continuously Variable Timing | 0–100mph | 6.5secs | | | Length | 4702mm/185in |
| | | Maximum Speed | 217mph + | | | Width | 2035mm/80in |
| Displacement | 5988cc | Steering | Rack & Pinion with power assist | Suspension Front | Double wishbones with pushrod links, coil springs, gas dampers & anti-roll bar | Height | 1147mm/45in |
| Maximum Power | 660bhp at 7,800rpm | | | | | Wheels Front | 9 x 19in |
| Maximum Torque | 485lb ft at 5,500rpm | Brakes Front | Ventilated carbon-ceramic discs with 6-pot callipers, ABS/380mm/15mm | Suspension Rear | Double wishbones with pushrod links, coil springs, gas dampers & anti-rollbar | Wheel Rear | 12 x 19in |
| Transmission | Six-speed sequential gearbox | | | | | Price | £450,000/US$670,000 |

There's one prerequisite for a supercar – it has to go like hell; and like Hades goes the Koenigsegg. Made in Sweden, the Koenigsegg CC, the dark horse of the supercar world, first broke cover in 2000 and blew the socks and anoraks off the motoring world.

The car is the brainchild of Christian von Koenigsegg who set up the supercar project back in 1993 with a small, dedicated group of enthusiasts. From such humble beginnings emerged the record-breaking monster that you're looking at now. With its latest incarnations, the CC8S and the CCR, that power is now the stuff of legend – the top of the range CCR is officially the fastest production car in the world and can propel you to McLaren F1-vanquishing speeds of beyond 242mph.

*Ferociously fast, perfectly composed and luxurious... ladies and gentlemen, meet Sweden's McLaren F1 slayer with the world's most unpronounceable name...*

# Koenigsegg CC

But making a record-breaking car means precious little if the car can't handle such colossal power – thankfully though, Koenigsegg has done its homework here as well. The chassis, made from carbon fibre composite, is renowned for its communicative feedback whether the car's hurtling along at 200mph plus, or being threaded through pot-holed city streets. Then add in the factor that this

car is unflappable and perfectly composed on the road – it manages to mix suppleness with practically zero body roll. The end result is a driving experience that never makes the driver feel left out of the loop with what is going on underneath.

While the 'base' model – the CC8S – offers 655bhp, its big brother, the CCR launched in 2004, has a staggering 806bhp on tap and can make the dash from 0–62 in only 3.2secs. This 'extreme' version of the Koenigsegg is achieved by boosting the 'standard' 4.7-litre V8 engine with a bi-compressor centrifugal supercharging system.

You would expect with such explosive power in a hardcore form that you'd find the interior somewhat lacking – that the Koenigsegg options would be limited to a cassette player at best or a floor carpet at worst. Not so with this Swedish supercar – as well as a full leather interior and CD player, the driver can indulge in a wide range of luxuries such as GPS navigation, a rear-view camera, a telephone system and even bespoke suitcases (where you'd put those is another issue altogether). And for those drivers who like the feel of the wind through their hair, open-air thrills are also available because the car comes with a removable roof panel that can be stored under the front bonnet.

The Koenigsegg offers that rare blend of incredible but utterly exploitable power, and genuine luxury to make the drive of your life the most comfortable possible. Yes, the price tag of £407,000 plus (US price based on customer specification) is a huge amount of cash – but the Koenigsegg is worth every penny. A truly remarkable supercar and virtually unbeatable; never has the phrase 'from zero to hero' been quite so true.

## Full House

The Koenigsegg headquarters are housed in a large fighter jet facility and there are 30 full-time staff. At the moment, seven vehicles can be assembled simultaneously and one car – bearing in mind there are 300-plus carbon fibre parts per car – takes 1,000 hours to assemble.

## Door To Door

The carbon fibre doors of the CC open by swinging upwards and resting at a 90° angle. Thanks to gas struts, this operation can be done with a gentle push and also means that the car is easily accessible even in confined spaces.

## Record Breaker

In the 2004 edition of the *Guinness Book Of Records*, the Koenigsegg CC8S is listed as the most powerful production car on the face of the planet. This has now been smashed by the 806bhp CCR, which currently holds the world record for the planet's most powerful streetcar.

## Have Car, Wheel Travel

The five-spoke magnesium alloy rims featured on the CCR have been specifically designed for Koenigsegg, and the tyres are guaranteed to withstand the strains and stresses of travelling at over 240mph.

## Not Too Hot To Handle?

The engineers at Koenigsegg have implemented KACS (Koenigsegg Advanced Control System) as standard on the CCR – this allows the driver to adjust the car's suspension, aerodynamics, road holding and braking components for their preferred set-up.

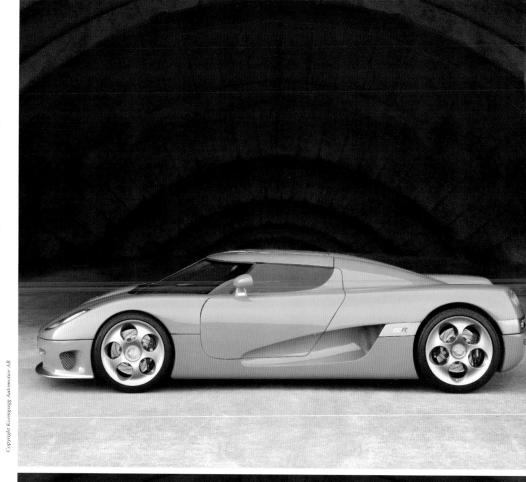

*Copyright Koenigsegg Automotive AB*

*Copyright Koenigsegg Automotive AB*

## Koenigsegg CCR: The Specifications

| | | | | | |
|---|---|---|---|---|---|
| Engine | V8 cast aluminium, supercharged | 0–1/4 miles | 9secs | Suspension Front | Double wishbones, adjustable VPS custom racing shock absorbers, pushrod operated & anti-roll bar |
| | | Maximum Speed | 242mph + | | |
| Valvetrain | DOHC 4 valves / cyl | Steering | Rack and pinion with power assist | | |
| Displacement | 4700cc | | | | |
| Maximum Power | 806bhp at 6,900rpm | Brakes Front | Ventilated with six-piston light alloy callipers, ABS/362mm/14in | Suspension Rear | Double wishbones, adjustable VPS custom racing shock absorbers, pushrod operated & anti-roll bar |
| Maximum Torque | 678lb ft at 5,700rpm | | | | |
| Transmission | Six-speed manual | | | | |
| 0–62mph | 3.2secs | Brakes Rear | Ventilated with six-piston callipers/362mm/14in | | |

| | |
|---|---|
| Kerb Weight | 1230kg/2711lb |
| Length | 4190mm/164in |
| Width | 1990mm/78in |
| Height | 1070mm/42in |
| Wheels Front | 9.5 x 19in |
| Wheel Rear | 12.5 x 20in |
| Price | £407,000/ US price based on customer specification |

*German build quality partnered with Italian passion... it's an intriguing concept but one that has paid off for the raging bull...*

There were some bated breaths in the car community when Audi bought out Lamborghini in 1998 – yes, the idea of a car manufacturer known for making bullet-proof pluto barges was a welcome one; perhaps they could temper the sometimes unforgiving nature of Lamborghini's previous cars such as the classic Diablo. But could such a company evolve the iconic supercar marque but keep what makes any Lamborghini so special – the rawness, and the sheer scariness. Or could we end up with a supercar that lacked a certain something? In other words, would the bull be tamed?

# Lamborghini Murcielago

All was revealed in 2001 when the result of Lamborghini's and Audi's mating rolled out in front of the public eye. But they need not have worried themselves.

The Murcielago is, yes, more refined and better built but don't start worrying that the Lamborghini has been sanitized. While Audi has ensured that the car has improved safety features and is better built than its predecessors, the Murcielago still has more than enough go to put a cold sweat on the foreheads of even the most experienced driver when taking the car to the limit.

The engine alone will see to that – with 580bhp, the aluminium 6.2-litre V12 is blisteringly quick, and with its four-wheel drive with a central vicious coupler plus traction control, the steel and carbon fibre-built Lamborghini's huge power can be placed down on the road with more ease than its predecessors. The Murcielago also represents a first for the Lamborghini with the inclusion of a six-speed manual gearbox. The car's rear spoiler adjusts depending on the

speed, and those fabulous air intakes mounted on the car's rear shoulders open and close to cool the mammoth engine. And for the show-offs, there's also a dash-mounted button to activate that 'Variable Air-flow Cooling System'.

Lamborghini purists may be slightly disappointed with the car's exterior – but while the aggressive, melodramatic styling of previous Lamborghinis looked like testosterone wrought in metal, the more subtle Murcielago still demands your attention with its clean, simple and muscular lines – it's a thoroughly modern reimagining of the Lamborghini spirit penned by Belgian designer Luc Donckerwolcke.

All this handling and visual drama is backed-up by Audi's obsession with build. The Murcielago was put through a series of punishing tests to make sure that its reliability was up to scratch – while the previous Diablo had only five prototypes racing round the Nardo race track and Sant'Agata in Italy, twelve Murcielagos were taken as far a field as the USA to see how they would bear up under such scorching and harsh temperatures.

It's with this new mindset – the passion of Lamborghini and the build quality of Audi – that the company has matured into a true 21st century supercar marque. With the arrival of the even more desirable and critically acclaimed Roadster version of the Murcielago, the bull is all set to bear down on its competition well into the future.

## What's In A Name?

The Murcielago is named after a bull that fought with the famous matador Rafael Molina 'Lagarttijo' on October 5, 1879. The afore-mentioned bull fought so bravely – and withstood being stabbed 24 times – that the great matador decided to honor the bull and spare its life. The bull was given to a top breeder and the Murcielago lineage continues to this day.

## Bullet Proof?

Build quality and reliability were issues that sometimes hovered over the Lamborghinis of old. The now Audi-owned company say that Murcielagos are being driven over 10,000 miles a year by some customers with no problems.

## Off With Its Head

Unlike the Diablo Roadster, which horrified the critics on its release, the Murcielago Roadster has taken their breaths away – not only incredible to look at but also a true zero-compromise supercar as well.

## All-Wheel Thrills

Lamborghini wanted all the Murcielago's power put firmly down on the road so the driver could enjoy it, and not simply destroy the car's tyres. Subsequently, any excess torque on the rear axle is moved to the front axle to aid the Murcielago get the best traction.

## *Lamborghini Murcielago: The Specifications*

| | | | | | |
|---|---|---|---|---|---|
| **Engine** | Aluminium alloy V12 | **Transmission** | Six-speed manual / Optional E-Gear | **Brakes Rear** | Vented Discs with 4-pot callipers, ABS/335mm |
| **Valvetrain** | DOHC, 4 valves / cyl with variable-geometry intake system and variable valve timing | **0–60mph** | 3.8secs | **Suspension Front** | Double wishbones with coil springs, gas dampers & anti-roll bar |
| | | **0–125mph** | 8.6secs | | |
| | | **Maximum Speed** | 205mph | | |
| **Displacement** | 6192cc | **Steering** | Rack & Pinion with power assist | **Suspension Rear** | Double wishbones with coil springs, gas dampers & anti-roll bar |
| **Maximum Power** | 580bhp at 7,500rpm | | | | |
| **Maximum Torque** | 479lb ft at 5,400rpm | **Brakes Front** | Vented discs with 4-pot callipers, ABS/355mm/14in | **Kerb Weight** | 1650kg/3638lbs |

| | |
|---|---|
| **Length** | 4580mm/180in |
| **Width** | 2045mm/80in |
| **Height** | 1135mm/45in |
| **Wheels Front** | 8.5 x 18in |
| **Wheel Rear** | 13 x 18in |
| **Price** | £162,000/US$228,000 |

*Exotic, outlandish, eccentric...
the Zonda is the most individual
supercar the world has ever seen...*

It looks more than modern – in fact, the Zonda looks like it could have been plucked straight from the pages of some sci-fi magazine, so vividly different does it look from its road-going competitors. But the origins of the car actually date back decades – after all, its Argentinean creator Horacio Pagani was only 12 when he first began making models of supercars from wood and moulded clay, and by the age of 20, he had already constructed his first race car for Renault.

# Pagani Zonda

Now firmly ensconced in the 21st century, the lucid teenage dreams of Horacio have managed to create what many argue is the world's finest supercar. First revealed at the Geneva Motor Show, Switzerland, in 1999, the prototype of the Zonda was always going to cause a fuss – with those alien looks, it simply couldn't fail not to.

But its extraordinary beauty isn't merely skin deep. It's worth bearing in mind that Horacio made a name for himself at Lamborghini before then heading off to create his own automobile design and engineering company, Modena Designs, in 1991, which specialized in lightweight composites. Always on the cards though was the Pagani supercar company and with Horacio's specialist knowledge, the Zonda has an impeccable pedigree.

Unsurprisingly then, at the heart of the car is its unique use of composite materials with a carbon fibre chassis and body, ensuring an incredibly lightweight and rigid structure. Add into that a bullet-proof, smooth-revving Mercedes-Benz AMG V12 – after all, those Germans know how to build a reliable engine that won't blow up when you're attempting to top 200mph. The original five-speed C12 had 389bhp on tap in 6.9-litre form and has been constantly evolving ever since. The six-speed Zonda C12 S which is shown here has now evolved into the S 7.3 – all 555bhp of it boasting a 0–60 time of 3.6secs. Traction control is included, which is mighty handy for nailing all that power to the road in wet conditions

Perhaps the most keenly anticipated Pagani was the 555bhp Roadster – but there was a genuine concern among fans that chopping off the roof of the Zonda would leave its handling horribly compromised. But again, Pagani and his team managed to blow away any concerns by introducing a new carbon fibre central chassis structure, and a roll bar made from carbon and chrome-molybdene to ensure that rigidity remained at the heart of the Zonda Roadster's winning formula.

The most extreme Zonda was introduced in 2005 – the F version. Built alongside the standard Zonda, it features a lighter chassis and better aerodynamics courtesy of a host of changes including a larger front splitter. That monster Mercedes engine is now even more powerful thanks to a new induction system which means you've got a whopping 602bhp under your right foot – the power-hungry driver wanting even more face-stretching acceleration can of course settle for the Clubsport edition that boasts 650bhp.

For all its firepower though, what makes the Zonda supercar truly exceptional is that while it can lap tracks with the best of them, it also boasts the comfort, and just as important, the reliability of a GT car.

The culmination of Horacio Pagani's dream is now a supercar that can hold its own when put up against the established names like Porsche, Lamborghini and Ferrari. And that is one hell of an achievement.

## Exclusivity Guaranteed

The Roadster is regarded as the most desirable of the Zonda range, so interested customers are recommended to put their money down quickly – after all, the Roadster's production will be capped at only 40.

## What's In A Name?

What's a supercar without a suitably evocative name? The word Zonda actually comes from a warm wind that blows west across the Andes Mountains in South America.

## In Good Company

The Zonda's creator Horacio Pagani had expert help from the now-deceased Grand Prix racing legend, Juan Manuel Fangio. He is credited with aiding Horacio with all aspects of the supercar's creation – from its styling to its world-class handling.

## Bespoke Heaven

The interior of the Zonda is as unique as its exterior with its mix of aluminium, leather and carbon fibre. Of course, for that special supercar touch, the company also provides owners with bespoke leather luggage and a pair of driving shoes with every car.

## Leap Of Faith

Talk about conviction – Horacio Pagani was so sure that the Zonda would be a hit with the public once they'd seen it at the 1999 Geneva Motor Show, that he'd already had the car crash tested and ramped up ready for production. His instincts proved correct – only months after its unveiling, he had enough orders to take up two years' worth of the car's production.